The Ultimate

VEGETABLE

Recipe Book

By

Celeste Jarabese

DISCLAIMER

Content Arcade Publishing and its authors are joined together in their efforts in creating these pages and their publications. Content Arcade Publishing and its authors make no assurance of any kind, stated or implied, with respect to the information provided.

LIMITS OF LIABILITY

Content Arcade Publishing and its authors shall not be held legally responsible in the event of incidental or consequential damages in line with, or arising out of, the supplying of the information presented here.

TABLE OF CONTENTS

INTRODUCTION

This book covers sumptuous vegetable recipes from classic to something extraordinary.

With the increasing number of people who are suffering from different kinds of illness brought about by a faulty diet, many are now are turning to plant-based food sources to reverse their health conditions.

Some very busy people may have neglected the importance of eating vegetables, especially the ones who ate at fast food almost every day. Now, if you are one of them this is the perfect time to change your eating habits and learn to eat healthily by incorporating vegetables into your daily meals.

This book is a compilation of easy to cook vegetable recipes that you and your family will surely love. The recipe ingredients call for natural foods with high nutritive value. This will help in ensuring that you get your daily source for dietary fiber, important vitamins and minerals, as well as antioxidants.

Also included here are some smart tips on buying, prepping, and cooking vegetable dishes.

This book is a part of many cookbook series that I am writing, I hope you have fun trying all the recipes in this book.

So now, let's get it started!

Tips For Buying Preparing, And Cooking Your Vegetables

BUYING

- **Spend wisely** - buy vegetables that are in season, it is more cost efficient than those that are not in season.

- **Choose quality** – buying vegetables that are fresh and have good quality is most definitely the best option. Processed vegetables often have high sodium and/or fat content. Whenever possible, go for organic farm produce to get maximum health benefits.

- **Look for firm and free from spots** - buy firm and heavy vegetables without soft or brown spots.

- **Avoid wilts** - when buying your leafy vegetables, make sure that the leaves are not wilted, deep green in color, and crisp.

- ***Heavy is good***-Choose cruciferous vegetables such as cabbage and lettuce heads that are heavy and firm. They are also economical since they can be bought per piece and not by weight. This way you get to have more at the same cost.
- ***Brighter color is better***-when buying vegetables you should look for brightly colored produce like tomatoes, eggplants, and peppers.

PREPPING

- It is always best to rinse your veggies before peeling and cutting them. Doing it the other way would lead to loss of nutrients.
- Rinsing your veggies thoroughly in running water will ensure they are free from

dust, sand, and any chemical spray residue.

- Most vegetables are highly perishable or have shorter shelf life - use them early because quality decline with time.

COOKING

- To maximize health benefits, do not overcook your vegetables because there are certain nutrients that are not stable to heat.
- Use of aromatics like garlic, onion, spices, and herbs can enhance the flavor of your dish.

Easy Vegetarian Wok Stir-Fry

This Asian-style stir-fried vegetables is packed with goodness in every bite.

Preparation Time: 10 minutes
Total Time: 20 minutes
Yield: 4-6 servings

Ingredients
2 Tbsp. vegetable oil

1 large red onion, sliced
½ teaspoon garlic, crushed
2 cups broccoli, cut into florets
1 cup snow peas or snap peas, trimmed
1 cup green beans, cut into 2-inch pieces
1 medium yellow bell pepper, cut into strips
1 medium carrot, cut into thin strips
¼ cup vegetable stock or chicken stock
2 tablespoons soy sauce
1 teaspoon sesame oil
salt and freshly ground black pepper

Method

1. Heat oil in a wok over medium-high heat. Stir-frythe onion and garlic for 1 minute.
2. Add broccoli, snap peas, green beans, bell pepper, carrot, stock, and soy sauce. Cook for about 7-8 minutes or until tender but still crisp, stirring frequently. Season with salt and pepper to taste. Stir in sesame oil.Remove from heat.
3. Transfer to a serving platter.
4. Serve and enjoy.

Sauteed Cabbage Mushroom and Pepper

This sautéed vegetable recipe made with cabbage, mushrooms, and pepper is not only delicious but nutritious too!

Preparation Time: 10 minutes
Total Time: 25 minutes
Yield: 4-6 servings

Ingredients
2 tablespoonsvegetable oil

2 shallots, sliced
1 teaspoon garlic, minced
1 medium head cabbage, shredded
1 cup button mushrooms, sliced
1 medium red bell pepper, cut into strips
2 tablespoons rice vinegar
2 tablespoons soy sauce
salt and freshly ground black pepper

Method

1. Heat oil in a wok over medium-high heat. Sautéshallots and garlic for 1 minute.
2. Add the cabbage, mushrooms, red bell pepper, and cilantro. Cook for about 5-7 minutes, stirring frequently.
3. Stir in rice vinegar and soy sauce, cook further 2 minutes. Season with salt and pepper to taste. Remove from heat.
4. Transfer to a serving dish.
5. Serve and enjoy.

Herbed Garlic Mushroom Stir-Fry

This simple Vegetarian-friendly recipe only calls for 5 basic ingredients.

Preparation Time: 5 minutes
Total Time: 15 minutes
Yield: 3-4 servings

Ingredients

1 tablespoon butter
1 teaspoon olive oil

1 teaspoon garlic, minced
2 cups button mushrooms, whole
¼ cup fresh parsley, chopped

Method

1. In a large skillet or non-stick pan, heat butter and oil over medium heat. Stir-fry garlic until aromatic.
2. Add button mushrooms and parsley. Cook, stirring for 5-7 minutes.
3. Transfer to a serving dish.
4. Serve and enjoy.

Stir-Fried Mixed Vegetable with Beef Strips

This quick stir-fry made with mixed veggies and beef strips is really delicious.

Preparation Time: 10 minutes
Total Time: 20 minutes
Yield:4-6 servings

Ingredients

2 Tbsp. vegetable oil
1 medium onion, sliced thin
1 teaspoon garlic, minced
1 pound sirloin beef, cut into thin strips
1 cup button mushrooms, sliced thinly
1 small head broccoli, cut into small florets
1 medium yellow bell pepper (capsicum), cut into strips
1 medium carrot, cut into thin strips
2 Tbsp. oyster sauce
2 Tbsp. rice vinegar
salt and freshly ground black pepper to taste

Method

1. In a large skillet or wok,heat oil over medium-high heat. Stir-fry onion and garlic for 1 minute.

2. Add beef strips and cook for 3-5 minutes or until browned, stirring frequently.

3. Addbroccoli, mushrooms, bell pepper, carrot, oyster sauce, and vinegar. Cover and cook further 5-7 minutes, stirring occasionally.

Season with salt and pepper, to taste.
4. Transfer to a serving dish.
5. Serve and enjoy.

Mixed Vegetable and Rice Combo

This awesome recipe with mixed vegetables and rice makes a great one-dish meal for lunch or dinner.

Preparation Time: 10 minutes
Total Time: 25 minutes
Yield: 4-5 servings

Ingredients
2 tablespoons olive oil

1 medium onion, chopped
1 medium carrot, diced
1 medium red bell pepper, diced
1 cup canned corn kernels, drained
1 cup frozen green peas, thawed
2 cups steamed rice
½ cup vegetable or chicken stock
1 teaspoon sesame oil
salt and freshly ground black pepper

Method

1. Heat oil in a non-stick pan or skillet over medium-high heat. Stir-fry onion and garlic for 1 minute.
2. Add carrot, bell pepper, corn kernels, and green peas. Cook for about 5-7 minutes, stirring frequently. Add the steamed rice and stock. Cook further 5 minutes. Stir in sesame oil. Season with pepper to taste.
3. Transfer to a serving dish.
4. Serve and enjoy.

Chinese-Style Vegetable Stir-Fry

This simple dish is ideal for busy weeknights, so colorful and flavorful!

Preparation Time: 10 minutes
Total Time: 20 minutes
Yield: 3-4 servings

Ingredients
2 Tbsp. peanut oil
2 shallots, sliced thin

2 cloves garlic, minced
2 cups broccoli, cut into small florets
1 cup baby corn or young corn, halved
1 cup snap peas, trimmed
1 medium red bell pepper, cut into strips
2 tablespoons light soy sauce
1 teaspoon Worcestershire sauce
salt and freshly ground black pepper to taste

Method

1. In a large skillet or wok, heat peanut oil over medium heat. Stir-fry shallots and garlic for 1 minute or until aromatic.
2. Add the broccoli, baby corn, snap peas, and red bell pepper. Cook, stirring frequently for 5 minutes.
3. Stir in soy sauce and Worcestershire sauce. Cover and cook further 3-5 minutes, stirring occasionally. Season with salt and pepper, to taste.
4. Transfer in a serving dish.
5. Serve and enjoy.

Sesame Vegetable and Shrimp Stir-Fry

This tasty and healthy vegetable stir-fry with shrimp and sesame seeds is a dish that you can easily prepare during busy weeknights.

Preparation Time: 10 minutes
Total Time: 20 minutes
Yield: 4 servings

Ingredients
2 Tbsp. peanut oil, divided

8 oz. shrimps, peeled and deveined
1 medium onion, sliced thin
3 cloves garlic, minced
1 medium head broccoli, cut into small florets
1 medium red bell pepper, cut into strips
2 cups snap peas, trimmed
2 tablespoons light soy sauce
1 teaspoon Worcestershire sauce
salt and freshly ground black pepper to taste
toasted sesame seeds, to serve

Method

1. In a large frying pan or skillet, heat 1 tablespoon oil over medium-high heat. Cook the shrimps for 2-3 minutes, stirring frequently. Transfer to a plate.
2. Using the same skillet, heat remaining oil. Stir-fry onion and garlic until fragrant.
3. Add broccoli, bell pepper, and snap peas. Cook for 5-7 minutes, stirring occasionally. Stir in soy sauce and Worcestershire sauce. Season with salt and pepper to taste.

4. Transfer in a serving dish. Sprinkle with toasted sesame seeds.
5. Serve and enjoy.

Stir-Fried Bitter Melon with Egg and Tomato

This vegetable dish is popular in Asia, bitter melon is packed with nutrients like iron that is good for the health.

Preparation Time: 10 minutes
Total Time: 20 minutes
Yield: 2-3 servings

Ingredients
2 Tbsp. olive oil, divided

1 medium onion, thinly sliced
½ teaspoon garlic, minced
2medium tomatoes, sliced
1 medium bitter melon
1 medium carrot, cut into thin strips
1 large egg, beaten
salt and freshly ground black pepper

Method

1. Cut both ends of bitter melon then slice in half (lengthwise).Scoop out the seeds and white pith using a spoon. Slice thinly crosswise or diagonally, about 1/4-inch thick.

2. In a medium saucepan, bring water to a boil over medium-high heat. Add bitter melon and cook for 2-3 minutes. Remove from heat. Let sit for another 3 minutes. Drain. (This will help reduce the bitter taste)

3. Heatoil in a non-stick pan or skilletover medium-high heat. Stir-fry onion and garlic for 1 minute or until fragrant.

4. Add the tomatoes, bitter melon, and carrot. Cook for 7-8 minutes, stirring frequently.
5. Add the beaten egg.Cook further 3 minutes, stirring constantly. Season with salt and pepper to taste. Remove from heat.
6. Transfer to a serving dish.
7. Serve and enjoy.

Slow Cooker Spiced Bean Stew in Tomato Sauce

This is great slow cooker recipe that you should try on a weekend, simply dump everything in the slow cooker, do your chores and its ready when you get back.

Preparation Time: 5 hours 5 minutes
Total Time: 5 hours5 minutes
Yield: 4-5 servings

Ingredients

1 pound dry navy or pinto beans (soaked overnight, rinsed, and drained)
2 cups beef stock
1 ½ cup tomato sauce
¼ cup tomato paste
2 tsp. paprika
1 tsp. garlic powder
1 tsp. chili powder
1 tsp. caraway seeds
salt and freshly ground black pepper

Method

1. Place beans together with the beef stock, tomato sauce, tomato paste, paprika, garlic powder, chili powder, and caraway seeds in a slow cooker. Cover and cook on high for 5 hours. Season with salt and pepper, to taste.
2. Transfer to a serving dish.
3. Serve and enjoy.

Cheesy Mixed Vegetable Casserole

This cheesy vegetable casserole recipe is a perfect treat for brunch, lunch, or supper!

Preparation Time: 10 minutes
Total Time: 50 minutes
Yield: 6 servings

Ingredients
1 head broccoli, cut into small florets
1 head cauliflower, cut into small florets
1 cup button mushrooms, diced

1 medium carrot, diced
1 medium onion, diced
1 (10.75 ounce) can condensed cream of chicken soup
1 cup light mayonnaise
1 cup cheddar cheese, grated
1 teaspoon garlic powder
½ cup bread crumbs

Method

1. Preheat oven to 350 F.
2. In a large bowl, combine the broccoli, cauliflower, mushroom, carrot, onion, and garlic powder.
3. Stir in cream of chicken soup, mayonnaise and half of the cheese. Mix well.
4. Transfer mixture into a 9x13 inch baking dish. Sprinkle with remaining cheese and bread crumbs.
5. Bake in the oven for about 30 minutes, or until golden brown and bubbly.Cool slightly.
6. Serve and enjoy.

Roasted Mixed Vegetables with Herbs

This scrumptious roasted vegetables with a smoky, sweet, and herby flavor isgreat with steaks or baked poultry.

Preparation Time: 10 minutes
Total Time: 1 hour 55 minutes
Yield: 6 servings

Ingredients
1 medium zucchini, diced
1 pound baby potatoes

1 pound cherry tomatoes, halved
1 cup button mushrooms, halved
¼ cup red wine vinegar
2 tablespoons olive oil
1 Tbsp. fresh rosemary
1 teaspoon thyme, dried
1 teaspoon garlic powder
salt and freshly ground black pepper

Method

1. In a small bowl, whisk together red wine vinegar, olive oil, rosemary, thyme, and garlic powder.
2. Combine zucchini, baby potatoes, cherry tomatoes, and mushrooms in a baking dish. Drizzle with red wine vinegar mixture. Toss to coat. Cover and let sit for 1 hour to absorb flavors.
3. Preheat oven to 400 F.
4. Remove cover and toss the vegetables again. Season with salt and pepper to taste.
5. Bake in the oven uncovered for 20 minutes. Reduce heat to 300 F and cook further 15-20 minutes or until potatoes are tender.

6. Transfer to a serving dish.
7. Serve and enjoy.

Spicy Baked Potato Wedges

This spicy baked potato recipe is perfect with grilled steaksor you can eat it on its own.

Preparation Time: 5minutes
Total Time: 55 minutes
Yield:6 servings

Ingredients
2 lbs. baking potato, peeled and cut into wedges
2 Tbsp. olive oil

2Tbsp. butter, melted
1 tsp. cayenne pepper
1 tsp. paprika
½ tsp. cumin, ground
½ teaspoon garlic powder
¼ tsp. freshly ground black pepper

Method

1. In a small bowl, whisk together olive oil, butter, cayenne pepper, paprika, cumin, garlic powder, and pepper.
2. Place potatoes in a baking dish. Drizzle with oil-spice mixture. Toss to coat.
3. Preheat oven to 400 F.
4. Bake in the oven uncovered for 20 minutes. Reduce heat to 300 F and cook further 15-20 minutes or until potatoes are tender.
5. Transfer to a serving dish.
6. Serve and enjoy.

Cauliflower Broccoli and Cheese Casserole

This vegetable casserole recipe made with cauliflower, broccoli, herbs, and cheese is so delicious!

Preparation Time:10 minutes
Total Time:30 minutes
Yield:5-6 servings

Ingredients
1 head broccoli, cut into small florets
1 head cauliflower, cut into small florets
1 medium onion, diced

1 (10.75 ounce) can condensed cream of mushroom soup
1 cup light mayonnaise
2 Tbsp. Dijon mustard
½ tsp. dried tarragon
½ tsp. dried sage
1 teaspoon garlic powder
½ cup bread crumbs
½ cup cheddar cheese, grated
¼ cup mozzarella cheese, grated

Method

1. Preheat oven to 350 F.
2. In a large bowl, mix together cream of mushroom soup, mayonnaise, Dijon mustard, tarragon, sage, garlic powder, and bread crumbs.
3. Add the broccoli, cauliflower, and onion. Mix well.
4. Transfer mixture to a baking dish. Sprinkle with cheddar and mozzarella. Bake for 20 minutes. Cool slightly.
5. Serve and enjoy.

Baked Potato with Rosemary

This baked potato recipe with rosemary will make your meals more enjoyable.

Preparation Time: 10 minutes
Total Time: 4 hours 40 minutes
Yield: 4-6 servings

Ingredients

2 lbs. baking potato, peeled and cut into wedges
2 Tbsp. olive oil
2 Tbsp. butter, melted

1 Tbsp. fresh rosemary, chopped
1 teaspoon garlic powder
¼ tsp. freshly ground black pepper

Method

1. In a small bowl, whisk together olive oil, butter, rosemary, garlic powder, and pepper.
2. Place potatoes in a baking dish. Drizzle with oil-herb mixture. Toss to coat.
3. Preheat oven to 400 F.
4. Bake in the oven uncovered for 20 minutes. Reduce heat to 300 F and cook further 15-20 minutes or until potatoes are tender.
5. Transfer to a serving dish.
6. Serve and enjoy.

Arugula Avocado and Mango Salad with Walnuts

This vegetable salad recipe made with arugula, avocado, mango and walnuts is a fantastic meal in less than 15 minutes.

Preparation Time: 5 minutes
Total Time: 10 minutes
Yield: 4 servings

Ingredients

1 medium avocado, thinly sliced
1 medium ripe mango, thinly sliced

4 cups arugula or baby rocket
½ cup walnuts, coarsely chopped
¼ cup red wine vinegar
2 Tbsp. olive oil
salt and freshly ground black pepper

Method

1. In a large salad bowl, combine avocado, mango, and arugula. Drizzle with red wine vinegar and olive oil. Season with salt and pepper to taste. Toss gently to combine all ingredients.
2. Divide among 4 individual plates. Sprinkle with walnuts.
3. Serve and enjoy.

Easy Homemade Tabbouleh Salad

This Levantine-inspired recipe is very popular in many parts of the world because of its unique taste and aroma!

Preparation Time: 15 minutes
Total Time: 15 minutes
Yield: 4-6 servings

Ingredients

1 ½ cup cooked bulgur wheat
1 cup cucumber, diced
1 cup tomatoes, diced
1 cup flat-leaf parsley, chopped
1 cup mint leaves, chopped
1 cup green onion, chopped
salt and freshly ground black pepper

Lime Vinaigrette Dressing:

½ cup extra-virgin olive oil
¼ cup lime juice
1 Tbsp. honey
salt and freshly ground black pepper

Method

1. In a small bowl, whisk together olive oil, lime juice, and honey in a small glass bowl.
2. Combine the bulgur, cucumber, tomatoes, parsley, mint, and green onions in a large salad bowl. Drizzle with vinaigrette. Toss to combine. Season with salt and pepper, to taste.
3. Serve and enjoy.

Fresh Caprese Salad

This 5-ingredient Mediterranean salad recipe is can be made in a snap!

Preparation Time: 10 minutes
Total Time: 10 minutes
Yield: 4 servings

Ingredients

1 pound cherry tomatoes, halved
8 oz. fresh mozzarella balls
2 cups fresh sweet basil
salt and freshly ground black pepper

Balsamic Vinaigrette:
½ cup olive oil
2 Tbsp. balsamic vinegar
2 tsp. honey

Method
1. In a small bowl, whisk together olive oil, balsamic vinegar, and honey.
2. In a large bowl, combine cherry tomatoes, mozzarella and basil. Drizzle with prepared balsamic vinaigrette. Season with salt and pepper to taste. Toss to coat.
3. Serve and enjoy.

Fresh Garden Salad with Lemon-Herb Dressing

If you've got some garden vegetables around, this fresh salad recipe is the best way to use them up!

Preparation Time: 10 minutes
Total Time: 10 minutes
Yield: 4-5 servings

Ingredients
2 cups lettuce, torn
2 cups spinach

1 pound radish, thinly sliced
1 cup grape tomato, halved

Lemon-Herb Vinaigrette Dressing:
½ cup extra-virgin olive oil
2 Tbsp. lemon juice
2 tsp. Dijon mustard
1 tsp. fresh parsley, chopped
salt and freshly ground black pepper

Method

1. In a small bowl, whisk together olive oil, lemon juice, Dijon mustard, and parsley.
2. Combine the mango, lettuce, spinach, radish, and grape tomato in a large salad bowl. Season with salt and pepper, to taste. Toss to combine well.
3. Transfer in individual salad plates. Drizzle with prepared dressing.
4. Serve and enjoy.

Kale Edamame and Tomato Salad with Dried Cherries

This fantastic salad recipe with makes a filling lunch or dinner.

Preparation Time: 15 minutes
Total Time: 15 minutes
Yield: 4 servings

Ingredients
¼ cup balsamic vinegar
¼ cup extra-virgin olive oil

2 Tbsp.brown sugar
1/2 tsp.Koshersalt
1/2 tsp. ground black pepper
1 bunch Tuscan kale, stems removed and
leaves coarsely chopped
1 cup frozen shelled edamame
(soybeans), thawed
1 cup cherry tomatoes, halved
1 medium red onion, chopped
2/3 cup dried cherries

Method

1. In a small bowl, whisk together balsamic vinegar, olive oil, brown sugar, salt, and pepper until sugar is completely dissolved.Set aside.
2. Toss kale, edamame, cherry tomatoes, red onion, and dried cherries in a large bowl until combined well.
3. Transfer to individual plates. Drizzle with balsamic dressing.
4. Serve and enjoy.

Stir-fried Green Beansand Chicken Strips

This stir-fried green beans with chicken strips is a good way to meet your daily protein requirement.

Preparation Time: 10 minutes
Total Time: 20 minutes
Yield: 4 servings

Ingredients
2Tbsp. canola oil

2 shallot, chopped
2 cloves garlic, minced
1 lb. chicken breast fillet, cut into strips
10 oz. green beans, trimmed and cut into
2-inch pieces
2 Tbsp. light soy sauce
1 Tbsp. Worcestershire sauce
salt and freshly ground black pepper to
taste

Method

1. Heat oil in a large skillet over medium-high heat. Stir-fry shallot and garlic for 1 minute or until fragrant.
2. Add chicken and cook, stirring for 3-5 minutes or until browned.
3. Add green beans, soy sauce, and Worcestershire sauce. Sauté for 5-7 minutes, stirring occasionally. Season with salt and pepper to taste. Remove from heat.
4. Transfer in a serving platter.
5. Serve and enjoy.

Scrumptious Greek-Style Salad

This delightful salad recipe is everything you'd want to have in a quick meal.

Preparation Time:15 minutes
Total Time: 15 minutes
Yield:4-5 servings

Ingredients

1 head iceberg lettuce, torn
2 medium cucumber, thinly sliced
2 medium tomatoes, sliced
1 medium onion, sliced

¾ cup black olives
¾ cup feta cheese, herbed

Lemon Vinaigrette with Dill
½ cup extra virgin olive oil
¼ cup lemon juice
1 Tbsp. honey
1 tsp. fresh dill weed, chopped
salt and black pepper, to taste

Method
1. Whisk together olive oil, lemon juice, honey, and dill in a small bowl. Season with salt and pepper, to taste.
2. Combine iceberglettuce, cucumber, tomatoes, onion, olives, and feta cheese in a salad bowl. Toss to combine well.
3. Divide salad among individual plates. Drizzle with lemon vinaigrette with dill.
4. Serve and enjoy.

Kale Tomato and Blueberry Salad

This vegetable salad recipe made with kale, tomato, and blueberries is perfect for lunch, snack or light dinner.

Preparation Time: 10 minutes
Total Time: 10 minutes
Yield: 4 servings

Ingredients

1 bunch Tuscan kale, stems removed and leaves coarsely chopped
1 cup cherry tomatoes, halved

1 cup blueberries
¼ cup slivered almonds

Dressing:
¼ cup red wine vinegar
¼ cup extra-virgin olive oil
2 Tbsp. brown sugar
¼ tsp. Kosher salt
¼ tsp. ground black pepper

Method

1. In a small bowl, whisk together red wine vinegar, olive oil, brown sugar, salt, and pepper until sugar is dissolved. Set aside.
2. Toss kale, cherry tomatoes, and blueberries in a salad bowl until combined well.
3. Divide among 4 individual plates. Drizzle with balsamic dressing. Sprinkle with slivered almonds.
4. Serve and enjoy.

Vegetable and Seafood Sauté

This scrumptious vegetable stir-fry recipe with mixed seafood is perfect for a quick family dinner.

Preparation Time: 10 minutes
Total Time:25 minutes
Yield:4-5 servings

Ingredients
1 lb. asparagus, trimmed, cut into 2-inch pieces
1 medium carrot, cut into flowerets

½ lb. shrimps, peeled (deveined and tails intact)
½ lb. squid
2 Tbsp. vegetable oil
¼ cup scallions, chopped
2 cloves garlic, chopped
¼ cup dry white wine
2 Tbsp. light soy sauce
salt and freshly ground black pepper

Method

1. Clean the squid thoroughly and discard the skin. Cut in half(lengthwise), then lightly score the insides in a crisscross pattern. Cut into small pieces.
2. Heat 1 Tbsp. vegetable oil in a wok or large skillet over medium-high heat.
3. Sauté the squid and shrimp, cook for 2-3 minutes. Transfer to a clean plate.
4. Heat the remaining oil in the skillet, add the scallions andgarlic. Cook, stirring for 1 minute.

5. Add the asparagus and carrot. Stir-fry for 5-7 minutes or until they are crisp-tender.
6. Return the squid and shrimp to the skillet, add the wine and soy sauce. Stir-fry further 2-3 minutes or until heated through. Season with salt and pepper, to taste.
7. Transfer to a serving platter.
8. Serve immediately and enjoy.

Spinach Fig and Peach Salad

This wonderful salad recipe with baby spinach, fresh figs, and peaches is great for a healthy snack.

Preparation Time: 10 minutes
Total Time: 10 minutes
Yield: 4 servings

Ingredients

4 cups baby spinach
2 medium figs, thinly sliced

2 medium peaches, stoned and thinly
sliced

Dressing:
¼ cup extra-virgin olive oil
¼ cup lemon juice
1 Tbsp. honey
¼ tsp. Kosher salt
¼ tsp. ground black pepper

Method
1. In a small bowl, whisk together
   olive oil, lemon juice, honey, salt,
   and pepper. Set aside.
2. Toss the baby spinach, figs, and
   peaches in a salad bowl until
   combined.
3. Divide among 4 individual plates.
   Drizzle with dressing.
4. Serve and enjoy.

Spinach Strawberry and Almond Salad with Sesame

This fresh salad made with spinach, strawberries, almonds, andsesame seeds is rich in antioxidants and also packed with nice flavor.

Preparation Time: 10 minutes
Total Time: 10 minutes
Yield:4 servings

Ingredients
4 cups baby spinach

2 cups strawberries, halved
¼ cup slivered almonds
2 Tbsp. sesame seeds, toasted

Dressing:
¼ cup extra-virgin olive oil
¼ cup balsamic vinegar
1 Tbsp. honey
¼ tsp. Kosher salt
¼ tsp. ground black pepper

Method

1. In a small bowl, whisk together olive oil, balsamic vinegar, honey, salt, and pepper. Set aside.
2. Toss the baby spinach, strawberries, and slivered almonds in a salad bowl to combine.
3. Divide among 4 individual plates. Drizzle with dressing. Sprinkle with toasted sesame seeds.
4. Serve and enjoy.

Tuna Radish and Tomato Salad

A scrumptious vegetable and fish salad. It makes a great lunch or dinner for those people who are trying to lose weight because it is low in calories and high in fiber.

Preparation Time: 15 minutes
Total Time: 15 minutes
Yield: 4-6 servings

Ingredients
1 head lettuce, torn

½ lb. radish, thinly sliced
½ lb. asparagus, cut into 2-inch slices
1 cup canned tuna in water or oil, drained and flaked
1 cup kalamata olives
2 medium tomato, sliced

Dressing:
¼ cup extra-virgin olive oil
¼ cup red wine vinegar
1 Tbsp. agave nectar
¼ tsp. Kosher salt
¼ tsp. ground black pepper

Method

1. In a small bowl, whisk together olive oil, red wine vinegar, agave nectar, salt, and pepper. Set aside.
2. Toss the lettuce, radish, asparagus, tuna, olives, and tomato in a salad bowl to combine.
3. Divide salad among 4 individual plates. Drizzle with dressing.
4. Serve and enjoy.

Mixed Veggie and Bean Soup with Cilantro

This hearty vegetable soup recipe is a sure winner!

Preparation Time: 15 minutes
Total Time: 45 minutes
Yield: 4-6 servings

Ingredients
2 Tbsp. vegetable oil
1 medium red onion, sliced

1 tsp. garlic, minced
1 cup baked beans
1 medium carrot, diced
1 medium potato, diced
2 celery ribs, diced
2 cups chicken stock, home-prepared, unsalted
2 cups water
1 cup tomato puree
¼ cup fresh cilantro
salt and freshly ground black pepper

Method

1. In a large saucepan, heat oil over medium heat. Stir-fry onion and garlic until aromatic.
2. Add the baked beans, carrot, potato, baked beans, celery, chicken stock, water, tomato puree, and cilantro. Cover with lid and cook for 30 minutes or until vegetables are very tender. Season with salt and pepper to taste. Remove from heat.
3. Ladle in serving bowls.
4. Serve and enjoy.

Herbed Beetroot Soup with Sour Cream

This delightful soup recipe has its natural sweetness from the beetroot, very satisfying!

Preparation Time: 10 minutes
Total Time: 30 minutes
Yield:6 servings

Ingredients
1 Tbsp. canola oil
2 pcs. shallot, sliced

2 cloves garlic, minced
1 ½ lb. beetroot, cubed
1 tsp. cinnamon, ground
½ tsp. nutmeg
½ tsp. coriander seed, ground
2 cups vegetable stock
2 cups water
1 cup sour cream
salt and freshly ground black pepper

Method

1. In a large saucepan, stir-fry shallots and garlic for 1 minute or until aromatic over medium-high heat.
2. Add the beetroot, cinnamon, nutmeg, and coriander. Stir-fry for 3 minutes.
3. Add the stock and water. Bring to a boil. Reduce heat. Cover with lid and cook for 25 minutes, stirring occasionally. Remove from heat.
4. Transfer soup in a food processor or blender. Blend in batches, if needed. Return to saucepan. Cook over medium-high heat for 3 to 5

minutes. Season with salt and pepper to taste.

5. Ladle in serving bowls. Top with a dollop of sour cream. Garnish with parsley, if desired.

6. Serve and enjoy.

Herbed Broccoli Carrot and Onion Soup

This quick and easy soup recipe with broccoli, carrot, and onion is deliciously good for you because it contains fiber and other phytonutrients.

Preparation Time: 10 minutes
Total Time: 25 minutes
Yield:4 servings

Ingredients
2 Tbsp. olive oil
2 medium white onion, sliced

2 cloves garlic, minced
1 head broccoli, cut into florets
1 medium carrot, thinly sliced
1 celery rib, diced
2 cups chicken stock
2 cups water
½ tsp. dried thyme
½ tsp. dried parsley
salt and freshly ground black pepper

Method

1. In a large saucepan, stir-fry onion and garlic for 1-2 minutes or until aromatic over medium heat.

2. Add the broccoli, carrot, celery, chicken stock, water, thyme, and parsley. Bring to a boil. Reduce heat to a simmer and cover with lid.Cook for 15 minutes or until vegetables are tender. Season with salt and pepper to taste. Remove from heat.

3. Ladle in individual serving bowls.

4. Serve and enjoy.

Spiced Cream of Carrot Soup with Chives

If you are looking for a healthy and tasty soup that you can prepare in a snap, this is the recipe for you!

Preparation Time: 15 minutes
Total Time: 30 minutes
Yield: 4 servings

Ingredients
2 Tbsp. butter

½ cup red onion, sliced
2 cloves garlic, minced
1 lb. carrot, peeled and cut into small pieces
2 cups vegetable stock or chicken stock
2 cups water
1 tsp. paprika
1 cup half and half cream
¼ cup fresh chives, chopped
salt and freshly ground black pepper

Method

1. In a medium saucepan, melt butter and stir-fry onions and garlic for 1-2 minute or until aromatic over medium heat.

2. Add the carrots,vegetable stock, water, and paprika. Cover with lid and cook for 20 minutes or until tender, stirring occasionally. Remove from heat.

3. Transfer soup in a blender or food processor. Blend in batches, if necessary. Return mixture to saucepan.Stir in cream and cook further2-3. Season with salt and pepper to taste.

4. Ladle in serving bowls. Sprinkle with chopped chives.
5. Serve and enjoy.

Easy Home Gazpacho Soup

This delectable cold soup recipe made with tomatoes, avocado, cucumber, and herbs is nice to have around during hot season.

Preparation Time: 15 minutes
Total Time: 15 minutes
Yield: 4 servings

Ingredients

1 lb. medium tomatoes, cut into small pieces
1 medium avocado, cut into small pieces

1 medium cucumber, cut into small pieces
1 medium onion, chopped
2 cloves garlic, minced
2 celery ribs, diced
3 cups chicken stock
2 Tbsp. lime juice
1 Tbsp. fresh thyme, chopped
1 Tbsp. fresh parsley, chopped
½ tsp. cumin, ground
½ tsp. paprika
salt and freshly ground black pepper

Method

1. Place the tomatoes, avocado, cucumber, onion, garlic, and celery in a blender or food processor. Process until coarsely chopped. Transfer half of the vegetable mixture in a largenon-reactive bowl. Set aside.

2. Add the chicken stock, lime juice, thyme, and parsley in the blender with remaining mixture. Process until smooth. Pour the pureed vegetables into the large bowl. Season with salt and pepper, to

taste. Stir to combine well. Cover and chill until ready to serve.

3. Ladle in individual soup bowls. Garnish with fresh parsley, if desired.

4. Serve and enjoy.

Tofu Shiitake Mushroom and Green Onion Soup

This Asian-inspired soup recipe makes a comforting lunch or dinner when the weather gets cold.

Preparation Time: 10 minutes
Total Time: 30 minutes
Yield: 4-6 servings

Ingredients
1 Tbsp. peanut oil
1 medium onion

2 cloves garlic
1 tsp. ginger, grated
4 cups vegetable or chicken stock
1 cup water
2 cups firm tofu, cubed
2 oz. dried shiitake mushrooms, soaked in water, drained and thinly sliced
2 Tbsp. cornstarch
¼ cup water
1 tsp. sesame oil
¼ cup chopped green onion, to serve
salt and freshly ground black pepper

Method

1. Heat peanut oil in a large saucepan over medium-high heat. Stir-fry onion, garlic, and ginger for 1 minute or until aromatic.
2. Add stock and water. Bring to a boil.
3. Add the tofu and shiitake mushrooms. Cook for 10 minutes, stirring occasionally.
4. Meanwhile, combine cornstarch and ¼ cup water in a small bowl, stirring well to make a slurry.

5. Pour slurry into the soup and cook further 3 minutes, stirring constantly. Season with salt and pepper to taste.
6. Stir in sesame oil. Remove from heat.
7. Ladle in individual soup bowls. Sprinkle with green onions.
8. Serve and enjoy.

Tomato Soup with Croutons and Cheddar

Spice up your meal with this remarkable vegetable soup recipe made with tomatoes, croutons, and cheddar!

Preparation Time: 15 minutes
Total Time: 30 minutes
Yield: 4 servings

Ingredients

1 Tbsp. olive oil
¼ cup scallions, chopped

1 teaspoon garlic, minced
1 ½ lb. ripe tomatoes, sliced
2 celery ribs, diced
2 cups vegetable stock
1 cup water
1 tsp. dried basil
½ tsp. paprika
½ tsp. cumin, ground
½ tsp. coriander seed, ground
1 cup half and half cream
1 cup croutons
½ cup cheddar cheese, grated
salt and freshly ground black pepper

Method

1. In a large saucepan, stir-fry scallions and garlic for 1 minute or until aromatic over medium-high heat.

2. Add the tomatoes, celery, stock, water, basil, paprika, cumin, and coriander. Cover with lid and simmer for 15 minutes, stirring occasionally. Remove from heat.

3. Transfer soup in a food processor or blender. Blend in batches, if necessary. Return to saucepan, add

the milk and cook over medium-high heat for 3 to 5 minutes. Season with salt and pepper to taste.

4. Ladle in serving bowls. Top with croutons. Sprinkle with cheddar cheese.

5. Serve and enjoy.

Creamy Corn Soup with Paprika

Are looking for something to keep you warm on a cold winter night? Try this scrumptious corn soup recipe!

Preparation Time: 10 minutes
Total Time: 30 minutes
Yield: 4-6 servings

Ingredients

2 Tbsp. butter
1 medium white onion, sliced
1 tsp. garlic, minced

2 cups corn kernels
2 cups vegetable stock or chicken stock
1 cup half and half cream
1 tsp. paprika
salt and freshly ground black pepper
fresh parsley, for garnish

Method

1. Melt butter in a large saucepan over medium heat. Stir-fry onion and garlic for 1 minute or until fragrant.
2. Add the corn, stock and water. Bring to a boil. Reduce heat. Cover with lid and simmer for 15 minutes, stirring occasionally. Remove from heat.
3. Transfer soup in a food processor or blender. Pulse a few times to chop the corn. Return to saucepan, add the half and half cream and paprika. Cook over medium-high heat for 3-5 minutes. Season with salt and pepper to taste.
4. Ladle in serving bowls. Garnish with parsley.

5. Serve and enjoy.

Easy Quinoa and Potato Soup

This wonderful soup recipe with quinoais so easy to make and healthy!

Preparation Time: 10 minutes
Total Time: 40 minutes
Yield:4-5 servings

Ingredients
2 tablespoons olive oil
2 shallots, sliced
3 cloves garlic, minced
2 medium potatoes, diced

1 medium carrot, diced
1 medium red bell pepper, diced
4 cups chicken stock or beef stock
1 cup cooked white quinoa
3 tablespoons fresh coriander, chopped
salt and freshly ground black pepper, to taste

Method

1. Heat olive oil in a medium saucepan over medium-high heat. Stir-fry shallots and garlic for 1 minute or until fragrant.

2. Add the potatoes, carrot, bell pepper, and stock. Bring to a boil. Reduce heat.Cover and cook for 20 minutes or until the potatoes are tender.

3. Add quinoa and coriander. Cook further 10 minutes. Season with salt and pepper, to taste.

4. Ladle in individual bowls. Garnish with coriander leaves, if desired.

5. Serve and enjoy.

CreamyFresh Mushroom Soup

This cream-style soup with mushroomsis very filling and flavorful!

Preparation Time: 10 minutes
Total Time:30 minutes
Yield: 4 servings

Ingredients
1 Tbsp. butter
1 medium white onion, sliced
2 cloves garlic, minced
2 cups button mushrooms, sliced

1 cup dry white wine
2 cups vegetable stock, unsalted
1 cups water
1 cup half and half cream
½ tsp. dried tarragon
salt and freshly ground black pepper
chopped fresh parsley, to serve

Method

1. Heat butter in a medium saucepan over medium-high heat. Stir-fry onion and garlic for 1 minute or until fragrant.
2. Add the mushrooms and dry white wine. Cook for 2-3 minutes, stirring occasionally.
3. Stir in the stock and water. Bring to a boil. Reduce heat. Cover with lid and cook for 15 minutes.
4. Transfer mushroom soup in a food processor or blender, blend in batches if needed. Process until smooth. Return to saucepan. Add the half and half cream and tarragon, cook further 5 minutes, stirring frequently. Season with

salt and pepper to taste. Remove from heat.

5. Ladle in serving bowls. Garnish with parsley, if desired.

6. Serve and enjoy.

Lemony Lentil Soup with Herbs

This delicious lentil soup recipe with lemon and herbs is a great source of fiber and protein.

Preparation Time: 10 minutes
Total Time: 35 minutes
Yield: 4 servings

Ingredients
2 Tbsp. olive oil
1 medium red onion, sliced
1 teaspoon garlic, minced

2 cups lentil, cooked
2 celery stalks, diced
2 cups chicken stock or beef stock
2 cups water
½ tsp. dried parsley
½ tsp. dried thyme
salt and freshly ground black pepper

Method

1. Heat olive oil in a large saucepan over medium-high heat. Stir-fry onion and garlic until fragrant and onion become translucent.
2. Add the lentils, celery, stock, water, parsley, and thyme. Bring to a boil. Reduce heat. Cover and cook further 25 minutes. Season with salt and pepper, to taste.
3. Ladle in individual serving bowls.
4. Serve and enjoy.

Easy Homemade Pesto Sauce

This awesome pasta sauce recipe has a nice blend of flavors, just toss with some cooked pasta and your meal is ready!

Preparation Time: 10 minutes
Total Time: 10 minutes
Yield: 5-6 servings

Ingredients

4 cups fresh basil
4 cloves garlic, peeled
1 cup olive oil

¼ cup pine nuts
¼ cup cashew nuts
¼ cup parmesan cheese, grated
salt and freshly ground black pepper

Method

1. Combine basil, garlic, pine nuts, cashew nuts, and parmesan cheese in a food processor or blender. Process for 1-2 minutes. While machine is on, gradually pour in the olive oil.
2. Transfer pesto sauce in a serving dish.
3. Serve with pasta and enjoy.

Healthy Tomato Puree with Herbs

This homemade tomato puree with mixed herbs is the perfect recipe to make use of garden fresh tomatoes.

Preparation Time: 15 minutes
Total Time: 25 minutes
Yield: 4 servings

Ingredients

2 lbs. plum tomatoes
½ teaspoon dried oregano

½ teaspoon dried basil
salt and freshly ground black pepper
fresh parsley, for garnish

Method

1. Bring water in a medium saucepan to a boil. Remove from heat.
2. Add tomatoes and let sit for 5-7 minutes. Drain water.
3. Peel tomatoes and remove seeds. Place them in a food processor or blender and process for 30 seconds.
4. Pour pureed tomatoes in a medium saucepan and add herbs. Cook over medium heat for 10-15 minutes. Season with salt and pepper to taste. Remove from heat.
5. Your tomato puree with herbs is now ready to use.

Spicy Red Pesto Sauce

This red pesto sauce recipe with roasted tomatoes, bell pepper, and garlic is the perfect alternative tothe traditional basil pesto.

Preparation Time: 30 minutes
Total Time:30 minutes
Yield: 5-6 servings

Ingredients
1 lb. plum tomatoes
2 medium red bell pepper
4 garlic cloves

½ cup walnuts
¼ cup parmesan cheese, grated
½ teaspoon Italian seasoning
1 cup extra-virgin olive oil
salt and freshly ground black pepper

Method

1. Preheat broiler to high.
2. Combine tomatoes, red bell pepper, and garlic in a baking dish. Drizzle with 2 tablespoons olive oil. Place in the broiler and cook for 10 minutes. Let cool.
3. Peel the vegetables and put in a food processor or blender.
4. Add walnuts, parmesan cheese, and Italian seasoning. Process for 1-2 minutes. While machine is running, gradually pour in the olive oil. Season with salt and pepper to taste.
5. Transfer to a serving dish.
6. Serve with your choice of pasta and enjoy.

Creamy Mashed Potato with Garlic Chives

This awesome mashed potato recipe is so creamy and filling, best served with grilled steaks.

Preparation Time: 15 minutes
Total Time: 15 minutes
Yield: 5-6 servings

Ingredients

2 pounds potatoes, boiled, peeled and quartered

2 tablespoons butter
2/3cup milk
½ cup half and half cream
¼ cup fresh garlic chives, minced
salt and freshly ground black pepper

Method
1. Mash potatoes in a large bowl with butter using a potato masher.
2. Add milk and half and half cream gradually.
3. Add chives and mix well. Season with salt and pepper to taste.
4. Serve immediately and enjoy.

Easy Homemade Roasted Garlic

A simple trick such as adding some roasted garlic into your dishes makes them more flavorful. Go ahead and try this recipe!

Preparation Time: 5 minutes
Total Time: 25 minutes
Yield: 10 servings

Ingredients

1 lb. garlic bulbs
¼ cup olive oil

Method

1. Preheat oven to 300 F.
2. Cut the tops of each garlic bulb. Brush with olive oil and place in a baking dish.
3. Roast garlic for about 20 minutes. Let cool.
4. That's it! Your roasted garlic is now ready to use.

Pasta with Chicken Ham Asparagus and Cherry Tomatoes

When things get busy, this is adelightful and easy way to serve dinner to the whole family!

Preparation Time: 15 minutes
Total Time: 30 minutes
Yield: 4 servings

Ingredients

1 lb. spaghetti, dry
¼ cup olive oil
1 medium onion, chopped

1 teaspoon garlic, chopped
1 cup asparagus tips
1 cup cherry tomatoes, halved
1 cup stewed tomatoes
1 cup dry white wine
8 oz. chicken ham, cut into strips
½ teaspoon Italian seasoning
¼ cup grated parmesan cheese, to serve
salt and freshly ground black pepper
fresh parsley, for garnish

Method

1. Cook pasta as directed in the package instructions. Drain. Set aside.
2. Heat oil in a medium saucepan over medium-high heat. Stir-fry onion and garlic for 1 minute.
3. Add theasparagus tips,cherry tomatoes, stewed tomatoes, wine, and Italian seasoning. Cook for 5-7 minutes.
4. Add the chicken ham. Cook further 3-5 minutes. Season with salt and pepper, to taste.
5. Addthe cooked spaghetti and toss to combine.

6. Transfer to individual plates. Sprinkle with parmesan cheese and garnish with fresh parsley.
7. Serve immediately and enjoy.

Zucchini and Mushroom Lasagna

This Vegetarian pasta recipe with zucchini and mushroom is a great substitute to your usual pasta with meat sauce.

Preparation Time: 15 minutes
Total Time: 30 minutes
Yield: 4-5 servings

Ingredients

2 tablespoons olive oil
1 large onion, chopped
2 cloves garlic, minced
1 medium zucchini, thinly sliced

2 cups sliced mushrooms
¼ cup sliced black olives
2 cups tomato sauce
¼ teaspoon dried oregano
¼ teaspoon dried parsley
¼ teaspoon dried basil
1 cup fat-free ricotta cheese
½ cup silken tofu
1 lb. whole wheat lasagna noodles, dry
8 oz. fat-free mozzarella
grated parmesan cheese, to serve
salt and freshly ground black pepper
fresh parsley, for garnish

Method

1. Preheat oven at 180 C or 350 F.

2. Bring a large pot of salted water to a boil. Cook lasagna noodles for about 10-12 minutes. Drain. Set aside.

3. Heat oil in skillet over medium-high heat. Stir-fry onion and garlic until fragrant.

4. Add the zucchini, mushrooms, and black olives.Cook for about 3-5 minutes.

5. Mix together tomato sauce and herbs in a medium bowl.

6. Combine ricotta and tofu in a separate bowl.

7. Make layers of lasagna noodles, vegetable stir-fry, tomato sauce, and ricotta mixture in a baking dish. Sprinkle with parmesan cheese and mozzarella cheese. Bake for 20 minutes. Remove from heat. Garnish with fresh basil.

8. Serve immediately and enjoy.

Cheesy Quinoa Patties with Chives

Enjoy this Vegetarian-friendly burger recipe. It is made with quinoa, cottage cheese, and chives!

Preparation Time: 15 minutes
Total Time: 25 minutes
Yield: 4-6 servings

Ingredients

½ cup white quinoa, rinsed
1 cup water

¼ cup breadcrumbs
¼ cup rolled oats
2 whole eggs, lightly beaten
2/3 cup cottage cheese
1 medium onion, chopped
2 cloves garlic, minced
¼ cup fresh chives, chopped
Vegetable oil, for frying
salt and freshly ground black pepper, to
taste

Method

1. Mix together water and quinoa in a small saucepan. Bring to the boil over medium heat. Reduce the heat to low. Cover and simmer for 12-15 minutes or until the liquid is absorbed. Let cool.
2. Combine the cooked quinoa, breadcrumbs, oats, eggs, onion, garlic, and chives in a mixing bowl. Season with salt and pepper to taste. Cover and place in the refrigerator for 10-15 minutes. Form mixture (about 1/4 cup) into patties.

3. Heat oil in a large skillet ornon-stick frying pan over medium-high heat. Fry the quinoa patties for about 3 minutes on each side or until golden brown. Repeat procedure with the remaining uncooked patties.

4. Transfer to a serving plate.

5. Serve and enjoy.

Easy Quinoa Salad Supreme

This quinoa salad recipe with avocado, black beans, and corn is so delicious and can be made in just a few minutes!

Preparation Time: 15 minutes
Total Time: 15 minutes
Yield: 4 servings

Ingredients
2 cups cooked quinoa
1 cup cherry tomatoes, halved
1 cup avocado, diced
1 cup corn kernels, drained

¼ cup canned black beans, rinsed and drained
1 medium white onion, chopped
¼ cup fresh mint leaves
¼ cup lime juice
2 tablespoons extra-virgin olive oil
salt and freshly ground black pepper, to taste

Method

1. Place the quinoa, cherry tomatoes, avocado, corn kernels, black beans, onion, and mint in a large salad bowl. Drizzle with lime juice and olive oil. Season with salt and pepper to taste.Tossmixture to combine well.
2. Transfer to a serving dish.
3. Serve and enjoy.

Weight Loss Veggie Drink

This vegetable drink recipe can help you lose weight in no time because it is loaded with fiber and important nutrients that can help burn fat.

Preparation Time: 5 minutes
Total Time: 5 minutes
Yield: 2 servings

Ingredients
2 medium carrot, cut into small pieces

2 celery stalks, cut into small pieces
1 cup cherry tomatoes
1 cup coconut water

Method

1. Combine carrots, celery, cherry tomatoes, and coconut water in a high speed blender. Process until smooth.
2. Pour in 2 chilled glasses.
3. Serve and enjoy.

BeetrootTomato and Carrot Blast

Try this awesome drink made with beetroot, tomato, and carrot, this is so good!

Preparation Time: 5 minutes
Total Time: 5 minutes
Yield: 2 servings

Ingredients
2 medium beetroot, cut into small pieces
1 medium tomato, cut into small pieces
1 cup carrot juice

3-4 ice cubes

Method

1. Combine beetroot, tomato, carrot juice, and ice cubes in a high speed blender. Process until smooth.
2. Pour in 2 chilled glasses.
3. Serve and enjoy.

Cucumber Radish and Parsley Smoothie

This healthy drink will give you a good dose of vitamins, minerals, and antioxidants.

Preparation Time: 5 minutes
Total Time: 5 minutes
Yield: 2 servings

Ingredients

1 medium cucumber, peeled and cut into small pieces

1 medium apple, cored, peeled and cut
into small pieces
1 medium radish, cut into small pieces
½ cup radish leaves, chopped
½ cup coconut water
1 Tbsp. honey or agave nectar

Method

1. Combine cucumber, apple, radish, radish leaves, water, and honey in a high speed blender. Process until smooth.
2. Pour in 2 chilled glasses.
3. Serve and enjoy.

Healthy Veggie Mix Super Smoothie

So quick, tasty, and easy to prepare Vegan-friendly smoothie recipe!

Preparation Time: 10 minutes
Total Time: 20 minutes
Yield: 4 servings

Ingredients

3 medium beetroot, cut into small pieces
1 medium carrot, cut into small pieces

1 medium cucumber, peeled and cut into small pieces
1 medium apple, cored, peeled and cut into small pieces
1 cup broccoli, cut into small florets
1 celery stalk, cut into small pieces
1 (1-inch) fresh ginger, sliced
2 cups coconut water

Method

1. Place beetroot, carrot, cucumber, apple, broccoli, celery, ginger, and coconut water in a high speed blender. Process until smooth.
2. Pour in 4 chilled glasses.
3. Serve and enjoy.

Broccoli Apple Kiwi and Lettuce Smoothie

This green smoothie recipe has health promoting nutrients that can revitalize the body.

Preparation Time: 5 minutes
Total Time: 5 minutes
Yield: 4 servings

Ingredients
2 cups broccoli florets

2 medium green apple, cored, peeled, and cut into small pieces
2 medium kiwi fruit, cut into small pieces
2 lettuce leaves, shredded
2 ½ cups coconut water

Method

1. Place broccoli, apple, kiwi fruit, lettuce, and coconut water in a high speed blender. Process until smooth.
2. Pour in 4 chilled glasses.
3. Serve and enjoy.

Made in the USA
Monee, IL
24 June 2022